Ketogenic Diet Recipes

An All-Inclusive Walkthrough To Understand What A Low Carb Diet Means And Watch The Weight Drop Off With Healthy Cooking

Table of contents

7

WHAT IS A KETO DiET?

A keto diet is well known for being a low carb diet, where the body produces ketones in the liver to be used as energy. It's referred to as many different names – ketogenic diet, low carb diet, low carb high fat (LCHF), etc.

When you eat something high in carbs, your body will produce glucose and insulin.

Glucose is the easiest molecule for your body to convert and use as energy so that it will be chosen over any other energy source.

Insulin is produced to process the glucose in your bloodstream by taking it around the body.

Since the glucose is being used as a primary energy, your fats are not needed and are therefore stored. Typically on a normal, higher carbohydrate diet, the body will use glucose as the main form of energy. By lowering the intake of carbs, the body is induced into a state known as ketosis.

Ketosis is a natural process the body initiates to help us survive when food intake is low. During this state, we produce ketones, which are produced from the breakdown of fats in the liver.

The end goal of a properly maintained keto diet is to force your body into this metabolic state. We don't do this through starvation of calories but starvation of carbohydrates.

Our bodies are incredibly adaptive to what you put into it – when you overload it with fats and take away carbohydrates, it will begin to burn ketones as the primary energy source. Optimal ketone levels offer many health, weight loss, physical and mental performance benefits.

Benefits of a Ketogenic Diet

There are numerous benefits that come with being on keto: from weight loss and increased energy levels to therapeutic medical applications. Most anyone can safely benefit from eating a low-carb, high-fat diet.

Mental Focus

Many people use the ketogenic diet specifically for the increased mental performance.

Ketones are a great source of fuel for the brain. When you lower carb intake, you avoid big spikes in blood sugar. Together, this can result in improved focus and concentration.

Studies show that an increased intake of fatty acids can have impacting benefits to our brain's function.

Increased Energy & Normalized Hunger

By giving your body a better and more reliable energy source, you will feel more energized during the day. Fats are shown to be the most effective molecule to burn as fuel.

On top of that, fat is naturally more satisfying and ends up leaving us in a satiated ("full") state for longer.

Epilepsy

The ketogenic diet has been used since the early 1900's to treat epilepsy successfully. It is still one of the most widely used therapies for children who have uncontrolled epilepsy today.

One of the main benefits of the ketogenic diet and epilepsy is that it allows fewer medications to be used while still offering excellent control.

In the last few years, studies have also shown significant results in adults treated with keto as well.

Cholesterol & Blood Pressure

A keto diet has shown to improve triglyceride levels and cholesterol levels most associated with arterial buildup. More specifically low-carb, high-fat diets show a dramatic increase in HDL and decrease in LDL particle concentration compared to low-fat diets.

Many studies on low-carb diets show better improvement in blood pressure over other diets.

Some blood pressure issues are associated with excess weight, which is a bonus since keto tends to lead to weight loss.

Insulin Resistance

Insulin resistance can lead to type II diabetes if left unmanaged. An abundant amount of research shows that a low carb, ketogenic diet can help people lower their insulin levels to healthy ranges.

Even if you're athletic, you can benefit from insulin optimization on keto through eating foods high in omega-3 fatty acids.

Acne

It's common to experience improvements in your skin when you switch to a ketogenic diet.

For acne, it may be beneficial to reduce dairy intake and follow a strict skin cleaning regimen..

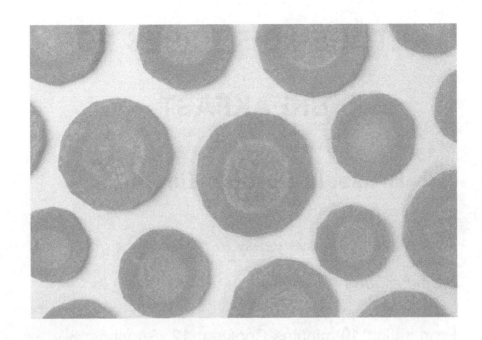

KETOGENIC RECIPES FOR

BREAKFAST

1. Brussels Sprouts Delight

This issotasty and veryeasy to make! It's a greatketo breakfast idea for you!

Preparation 10 minutes Cooking: 12 Servings: 3

Ingredients:

- 3 eggs Salt and black pepper to the taste

- 1 tablespoon ghee, melted

- 2 shallots, minced

- 2 garliccloves, minced

- 12 ounces Brussels sprouts, thinlysliced

- 2 ounces bacon, chopped

- 1 and   tablespoonsapplecidervinegar

Directions:

1. Heat up a pan over medium heat, add bacon, stir, cookuntilit'scrispy, transferto a plate and leaveaside for now.

2. Heat up the pan again over medium heat, addshallots and garlic, stir and cookfor 30 seconds.

3. Add Brussels sprouts, salt, pepper and applecidervinegar, stir and cook for 5minutes.

4. Return bacon to pan, stir and cook for 5 minutes more.

5. Add ghee, stir and make a hole in the center.

6. Crack eggsinto the pan, cookuntilthey are done and serve right away.

Nutrition:

- Calories 240 Fat 7 Fiber 4 Carbs 7
- Protein 12

2. Breakfast Cereal Nibs

Pay attention and learn how to prepare the best ketocerealnibs!

Preparation time: 10 minutes

Cooking time: 45minutes

Servings: 4

Ingredients:

- 4 tablespoonshemphearts
- cup chia seeds
- 1 cup water
- 1 tablespoonvanillaextract
- 1 tablespoon psyllium powder
- 2 tablespoonscoconutoil
- 1 tablespoonswerve
- 2 tablespoonscocoanibs

Directions:

1. In a bowl, mix chia seedswith water, stir and leaveaside for 5 minutes.

2. Addhemphearts, vanillaextract, psyllium powder, oil and swerve and stirwellwithyour mixer.

3. Addcocoanibs, and stiruntilyouobtain a dough.

4. Dividedoughin 2 pieces, shapeintocylinderform, place on a linedbakingsheet, flattenwell, cover with a parchmentpaper, introduce in the oven at 285degrees F and bake for 20 minutes.

5. Remove the parchmentpaper and bake for 25 minutes more.

6. Takecylinders out of the oven, leaveaside to cool down and cutintosmallpieces.

7. Serve in the morningwithsomealmondmilk.

Nutrition:

Calories 245 Fat 12 Fiber 12 Carbs 2 Protein 9

3. Breakfast Chia Pudding

Try a chia pudding thismorning!

Preparation time: 10 minutes

Cooking time: 30 minutes

Servings: 2

Ingredients:

- 2 tablespoons coffee
- 2 cups water 1/3 cup chia seeds
- 1 tablespoonswerve
- 1 tablespoonvanillaextract
- 2 tablespoonscocoanibs
- 1/3 cup coconutcream

Directions:

1. Heat up a small pot with the water over medium heat, bring to a boil, add coffee,simmer for 15

minutes, takeoffheat and straininto a bowl.

2. Addvanillaextract, coconutcream, swerve, cocoanibs and chia seeds, stirwell,keep in the fridge for 30 minutes, divideinto 2 breakfast bowls and serve.

Nutrition:

- Calories 100
- Fat 0.4
- Fiber 4
- Carbs 3
- Protein 3

4. Delicious Hemp Porridge

It's a hearty and 100% keto breakfast idea!

Preparation time: 3 minutes

Cooking time: 3 minutes

Servings: 1

Ingredients:

- 1 tablespoon chia seeds

- 1 cup almondmilk

- 2 tablespoonsflaxseeds

- cup hemphearts

- teaspooncinnamon, round

- 1 tablespoon stevia

- teaspoonvanillaextract

- cup almondflour

- 1 tablespoonhemphearts for serving

Directions:

1. In a pan, mix almondmilkwith   cup hemphearts, chia seeds, stevia, flaxseeds, cinnamon and vanillaextract, stirwell and heat up over medium heat.

2. Cook for 2 minutes, take off heat, addalmondflour, stirwell and pour intoabowl.

3. Top with 1 tablespoonhemphearts and serve.

Nutrition:

- Calories 230
- Fat 12
- Fiber 7
- Carbs 3
- Protein 43

5. Simple Breakfast Cereal

It'ssoeasy to make a tastyketo breakfast!

Preparation time: 10 minutes

Cooking time: 3 minutes

Servings: 2

Ingredients:

- cup coconut, shredded
- 4 teaspoons ghee
- 2 cups almondmilk
- 1 tablespoon stevia A pinch of salt
- 1/3 cup macadamia nuts, chopped
- 1/3 cup walnuts, chopped
- 1/3 cup flaxseed

Directions:

1. Heat up a pot with the ghee over medium heat,

addmilk, coconut, salt,macadamia nuts, walnuts, flaxseed and stevia and stirwell.

2. Cook for 3 minutes, stiragain, takeoffheat and leaveaside for 10 minutes.

3. Divideinto 2 bowls and serve.

Nutrition:

- Calories 140

- Fat 3

- Fiber 2

- Carbs 1.5

- Protein 7

6. Simple Egg Porridge

It'sso simple and tasty!

Preparation time: 10 minutes

Cooking time: 4 minutes

Servings: 2

Ingredients:

- 2 eggs
- 1 tablespoon stevia
- 1/3 cup heavycream
- 2 tablespoons ghee, melted
- A pinch of cinnamon, ground

Directions:

1. In a bowl, mix eggswith stevia and heavycream and whisk well.

2. Heat up a pan with the ghee over medium high heat, addegg mix and cookuntilthey are done.

3. Transfer to 2 bowls, sprinklecinnamon on top and serve.

Nutrition:

- Calories 340

- Fat 12

- Fiber 10

- Carbs 3

- Protein 14

KETOGENIC RECIPES FOR

LUNCH

7. Pumpkin Soup

This ketosoupisverycreamy and textured! You shouldreallytryit for lunch today!

Preparation time: 10 minutes

Cooking time: 20 minutes

Servings: 6

Ingredients:

- cup yellowonion, chopped

- 2 tablespoons olive oil

- 1 tablespoon chipotles in adobo sauce

- 1 garlicclove, minced

- 1 teaspoon cumin, ground

- 1 teaspooncoriander, ground

- A pinch of allspice

- 2 cups pumpkinpuree

- Salt and black pepper to the taste

- 32 ounceschicken stock

-     cup heavycream

- 2 teaspoonsvinegar

- 2 teaspoons stevia

Directions:

1. Heat up a pot with the oil over medium heat, addonions and garlic, stir and cookfor 4 minutes.

2. Add stevia, cumin, coriander, chipotles and cumin, stir and cook for 2 minutes.

3. Add stock and pumpkinpuree, stir and cook for 5 minutes.

4. Blend soupwellusing an immersion blender and then mix withsalt, pepper,heavycream and vinegar.

5. Stir, cook for 5 minutes more and divideinto bowls.

6. Serve right away.

Nutrition:

- Calories 140

- Fat 12

- Fiber 3

- Carbs 6

- Protein 2

8. Delicious Green Beans Casserole

This willimpressyou for sure!

Preparation time: 10 minutes

Cooking time: 35 minutes

Servings: 8

Ingredients:

- 1 pound green beans, halved
- Salt and black pepper to the taste
- cup almondflour
- 2 tablespoons ghee
- 8 ouncesmushrooms, chopped
- 4 ouncesonion, chopped
- 2 shallots, chopped
- 3 garliccloves, minced
- cup chicken stock
- cup heavycream

- cup parmesan, grated
- Avocadooil for frying

Directions:

1. Put some water in a pot, addsalt, bring to a boil over medium high heat, addgreenbeans, cook for 5 minutes, transfer to a bowl filledwithice water, cooldown, drain well and leaveaside for now.

2. In a bowl, mix shallotswithonions, almondflour, salt and pepper and tosstocoat.

3. Heat up a pan withsomeavocadooil over medium high heat, addonionsandshallots mix, fryuntilthey are golden.

4. Transfer to papertowels and drain grease.

5. Heat up the same pan over medium heat, add ghee and meltit.

6. Addgarlic and mushrooms, stir and cook for 5 minutes.

7. Add stock and heavycream, stir, bring to a boil and simmeruntilitthickens.

8. Add parmesan and green beans, toss to coat and take off heat.

9. Transfer this mix to a bakingdish, sprinklecrispyonions mix all over, introducein the oven at 400 degrees F and bake for 15 minutes.

10. Serve warm.

Nutrition:

- Calories 155
- Fat 11
- Fiber 6
- Carbs 8
- Protein 5

9. Simple Lunch Apple Salad

This is not justKetogenic! It'salsoverytasty!

Preparation time: 10 minutes

Cooking time: 0 minutes

Servings: 4

Ingredients:

- 2 cups broccoliflorets, roughlychopped
- 2 ounces pecans, chopped
- 1 apple, cored and grated
- 1 green onionstalk, finelychopped
- Salt and black pepper to the taste
- 2 teaspoonspoppyseeds
- 1 teaspoonapplecidervinegar
- cup mayonnaise
- teaspoonlemonjuice
- cup sourcream

Directions:

1. In a salad bowl, mix applewithbroccoli, green onion and pecans and stir.

2. Addpoppyseeds, salt and pepper and tossgently.

3. In a bowl, mix mayo withsourcream, vinegar and lemonjuice and whisk well.

4. Pour this over salad, toss to coatwell and serve cold for lunch!

Nutrition:

- Calories 250
- Fat 23
- Fiber 4
- Carbs 4
- Protein 5

10. Brussels Sprouts Gratin

It's a dense and richketo lunch idea!

Preparation time: 10 minutes

Cooking time: 35 minutes

Servings: 4

Ingredients:

- 2 ouncesonions, chopped

- 1 teaspoongarlic, minced

- 6 ounces Brussels sprouts, chopped

- 2 tablespoons ghee

- 1 tablespooncoconutaminos

- Salt and black pepper to the taste

- teaspoonliquidsmoke

For the sauce:

- 2.5 ounces cheddar cheese, grated

- A pinch of black pepper

- 1 tablespoon ghee

- cup heavycream

- teaspoonturmeric

- teaspoon paprika

- A pinch of xanthangum

For the porkcrust:

- 3 tablespoons parmesan

- 0.5 ouncesporkrinds

- teaspoonsweet paprika

Directions:

1. Heat up a pan with 2 tablespoons ghee over high heat, add Brussels sprouts, saltandpepper, stir and cook for 3 minutes.

2. Addgarlic and onion, stir and cook for 3 minutes more.

3. Addliquidsmoke and coconutaminos, stir, takeoffheat and leaveasidefornow.

4. Heat up another pan with 1 tablespoon ghee over medium heat, addheavycreamandstir.

5. Addcheese, black pepper, turmeric, paprika and xanthangum, stir and cookuntilitthickensagain.

6. Add Brussels sprouts mix, toss to coat and divideintoramekins.

7. In yourfood processor, mix parmesan withporkrinds and teaspoonpaprikaand pulse well.

8. Dividethesecrumbs on top of Brussels sprouts mix, introduceramekins in theoven at 375 degrees F and bake for 20 minutes.

9. Serve right away.

Nutrition:

Calories 300 Fat 20 Fiber 6 Carbs 5 Protein 10

KETOGENIC SIDE DISH

RECIPES

11. Amazing Coleslaw

Coleslaws are veryfamous! Today, werecommendyou a keto one!

Preparation time: 10 minutes

Cooking time: 0 minutes

Servings: 4

Ingredients:

- 1 small green cabbagehead, shredded
- Salt and black pepper to the taste
- 6 tablespoons mayonnaise
- Salt and black pepper to the taste
- 1 pinchfennelseed

- Juice from   lemon

- 1 tablespoon Dijon mustard

Directions:

1. In a bowl, mix cabbagewithsalt and lemonjuice, stirwell and leaveaside for 10minutes.

2. Presswell the cabbage, add more salt and pepper, fennelseed, mayo andmustard.

3. Toss to coat and serve.

Nutrition:

- Calories 150

- Fat 3

- Fiber 2

- Carbs 2

- Protein 7

12.   Simple Fried Cabbage

The cabbageissuch a versatile veggie! Try

thisamazingsidedish as soon as possible!

Preparation time: 10 minutes

Cooking time: 15 minutes

Servings: 4

Ingredients:

- 1 and   pound green cabbage, shredded
- Salt and black pepper to the taste
- 3.5 ounces ghee
- A pinch of sweet paprika

Directions:

1. Heat up a pan with the ghee over medium heat.

2. Addcabbage and cook for 15 minutes

   stirringoften.

3. Addsalt, pepper and paprika, stir, cook for 1 minute more, divide on plates andserve.

Nutrition:

- Calories 200
- Fat 4
- Fiber 2
- Carbs 3
- Protein 7

13. Delicious Green Beans And Avocado

Serve thiswith a tastyfishdish!

Preparation time: 10 minutesCooking time: 5 minutes

Servings: 4

Ingredients:

- 2/3 pound green beans, trimmed

- Salt and black pepper to the taste

- 3 tablespoons olive oil

- 2 avocados, pitted and peeled

- 5 scallions, chopped

- A handfulcilantro, chopped

Directions:

1. Heat up a pan with the oil over medium heat, add green beans, stir and cook for4 minutes.

2. Addsalt and pepper, stir, takeoffheat and transfer to a bowl.

3. In another bowl, mix avocadoswithsalt and pepper and mashwith a fork.

4. Addonions and stirwell.

5. Addthis over green beans, toss to coat and serve withchoppedcilantro on top.

Nutrition:

- calories 200

- fat 5

- fiber 3

- carbs 4

- protein 6

14.   Creamy Spaghetti Pasta

This isjustperfect for a turkeydish!

Preparation time: 10 minutes

Cooking time: 40 minutes

Servings: 4

Ingredients:

- 1 spaghetti squash
- Salt and black pepper to the taste
- 2 tablespoons ghee1 teaspoon Cajun seasoning
- A pinch of cayenne pepper
- 2 cups heavycream

Directions:

1. Prick spaghetti with a fork, place on a linedbakingsheet, introduce in the oven at 350degrees F and bake for 15 minutes.

2. Take spaghetti squash out of the oven, leaveaside to cool down a bit and scoop squashnoodles.

3. Heat up a pan with the ghee over medium heat, add spaghetti squash, stir and cook for acouple of minutes.

4. Addsalt, pepper, cayenne pepper and Cajun seasoning, stir and cook for 1 minute.

5. Addheavycream, stir, cook for 10 minutes more, divide on plates and serve as a ketosidedish.

Nutrition:

- Calories 200
- Fat 2
- Fiber 1
- Carbs 5
- Protein 8

15.   Amazing Roasted Olives

This is a greatsidedish! You'llsee!

Preparation time: 10 minutes

Cooking time: 20 minutes

Servings: 6

Ingredients:

- 1 cup black olives, pitted

- 1 cup kalamata olives, pitted

- 1 cup green olives, stuffedwithalmonds and garlic

-   cup olive oil

- 10 garliccloves

- 1 tablespoon herbes de Provence

- 1 teaspoonlemon zest, grated

- Black pepper to the taste

- Somechoppedthyme for serving

Directions:

1. Place black, kalamata and green olives on a linedbakingsheet, drizzleoil, garlicand herbes de Provence, toss to coat, introduce in the oven at 425 degrees F andbake for 10 minutes.

2. Stir olives and bake for 10 minutes more.

3. Divide olives on plates, sprinklelemon zest, black pepper and thyme on top, tosstocoat and serve warm.

Nutrition:

- Calories 200
- Fat 20
- Fiber 4
- Carbs 3
- Protein 1

16.   Delicious Veggie Noodles

These are verydelicious and incrediblycolored!

Preparation time: 10 minutes

Cooking time: 20 minutes

Servings: 6

Ingredients:

- 1 zucchini, cutwith a spiralizer
- 1 summer squash, cutwith a spiralizer
- 1 carrot, cutwith a spiralizer
- 1 sweetpotato, cutwith a spiralizer
- 4 ouncesredonion, chopped
- 6 ouncesyellow, orange and redbellpeppers, cut in thinstrips
- Salt and black pepper to the taste
- 4 tablespoons bacon fat
- 3 garliccloves, minced

Directions:

1. Spread zucchini noodles on a linedbakingsheet.

2. Add squash, carrot, sweetpotato, onion and all bellpeppers.

3. Addsalt, pepper and garlic and toss to coat.

4. Add bacon fat, tossagain all noodles, introduce in the oven at 400 degrees F andbake for 20 minutes.

5. Transfer to plates and serve right away as a ketosidedish.

Nutrition:

- Calories 50

- Fat 1

- Fiber 1

- Carbs 6

- Protein 2

KETOGENIC SNACKS AND APPETIZERS RECIPES

17. Simple Bread Sticks

You just have to givethisamazingketo snack a chance!

Preparation time: 10 minutes

Cooking time: 15 minutes Servings: 24

Ingredients:

- 3 tablespoonscreamcheese, soft

- 1 tablespoon psyllium powder   cup almondflour

- 2 cups mozzarella cheese, melted for 30 seconds in the microwave

- 1 teaspoonbakingpowder 1 egg

- 2 tablespoonsItalianseasoning

- Salt and black pepper to the taste

- 3 ounces cheddar cheese, grated

- 1 teaspoononionpowder

Directions:

1. In a bowl, mix psyllium powderwithalmondflour, bakingpowder, saltandpepper and whisk.

2. Addcreamcheese, melted mozzarella and egg and stirusingyour hands untilyouobtain a dough.

3. Spread this on a bakingsheet and cutinto 24 sticks.

4. Sprinkleonionpowder and Italianseasoning over them.

5. Top with cheddar cheese, introduce in the oven at 350 degrees F and bake for 15minutes.

6. Serve them as a keto snack!

Nutrition:

Calories 245 Fat 12 Fiber 5 Carbs 3 Protein 14

18.   ItalianMeatballs

This Italian style appetizeris 100% keto!

Preparation time: 10 minutes

Cooking time: 6 minutes

Servings: 16

Ingredients:

- 1 egg

- Salt and black pepper to the taste

-    cup almondflour

- 1 pound turkeymeat, ground

-    teaspoongarlicpowder

- 2 tablespoonssundriedtomatoes, chopped

-    cup mozzarella cheese, shredded

- 2 tablespoons olive oil

- 2 tablespoonbasil, chopped

Directions:

1. In a bowl, mix turkeywithsalt, pepper, egg, almondflour, garlicpowder, sundriedtomatoes, mozzarella and basil and stirwell.

2. Shape 12 meatballs, heat up a pan with the oil over medium high heat, dropmeatballs and cookthem for 2 minutes on eachside.

3. Arrange on a platter and serve.

Nutrition:

- Calories 80

- Fat 6

- Fiber 3

- Carbs 5

- Protein 7

19.   Parmesan Wings

Thesewillbeappreciated by all yourfamily!

Preparation time: 10 minutes

Cooking time: 24 minutes

Servings: 6

Ingredients:

- 6 pound chickenwings, cut in halves
- Salt and black pepper to the taste
- teaspoonItalianseasoning
- 2 tablespoons ghee
- cup parmesan cheese, grated
- A pinch of redpepper flakes, crushed
- 1 teaspoongarlicpowder 1 egg

Directions:

1. Arrange chickenwings on a linedbakingsheet,

introduce in the oven at 425degrees F and bake for 17 minutes.

2. Meanwhile, in your blender, mix ghee withcheese, egg, salt, pepper, pepperflakes, garlicpowder and Italianseasoning and blendverywell.

3. Takechickenwings out of the oven, flip them, turnoven to broil and broilthemfor 5 minutes more.

4. Takechickenpieces out of the ovenagain, pour sauce over them, toss to coatwell and broil for 1 minute more.

5. Serve them as a quick ketoappetizer.

Nutrition:

- Calories 134 Fat 8
- Fiber 1 Carbs 0.5
- Protein 14

20.   Cheese Sticks

This ketoappetizerwillsimplymeltintoyourmouth!

Preparation time: 1 hour and 10 minutes

Cooking time: 20 minutes

Servings: 16

Ingredients:

- 2 eggs, whisked
- Salt and black pepper to the taste
- 8 mozzarella cheese strings, cut in halves
- 1 cup parmesan, grated
- 1 tablespoonItalianseasoning
-    cup olive oil 1 garlicclove, minced

Directions:

1. In a bowl, mix parmesan withsalt, pepper,

   Italianseasoning and garlic and stirwell.

2. Put whiskedeggs in another bowl.

3. Dip mozzarella sticks in egg mixture, then in cheese mix.

4. Dipthemagain in egg and in the parmesan mix and keepthem in the freezer for1 hour.

5. Heat up a pan with the oil over medium high heat, addcheese sticks, frythemuntilthey are golden on one side, flip and cookthem the sameway on the otherside.

6. Arrange them on a platter and serve.

Nutrition:

- Calories 140

- Fat 5

- Fiber 1

- Carbs 3

- Protein 4

21.   TastyBroccoli Sticks

You must invite all yourfriends to taste

thisketoappetizer!

Preparation time: 10 minutes

Cooking time: 20 minutes

Servings: 20

Ingredients:

- 1 egg

- 2 cups broccoliflorets

- 1/3 cup cheddar cheese, grated

-    cup yellowonion, chopped

- 1/3 cup pankobreadcrumbs

- 1/3 cup Italianbreadcrumbs

- 2 tablespoonsparsley, chopped

- A drizzle of olive oil

- Salt and black pepper to the taste

Directions:

1. Heat up a pot with water over medium heat, addbroccoli, steam for 1 minute,drain, chop and put into a bowl.

2. Addegg, cheddar cheese, panko and Italianbreadcrumbs, salt, pepperandparsley and stireverythingwell.

3. Shape sticks out of this mix usingyour hands and place them on a bakingsheetwhichyou'vegreasedwithsome olive oil.

4. Introduce in the oven at 400 degrees F and bake for 20 minutes.

5. Arrange on a platter and serve.

Nutrition:

- Calories 100 Fat 4 Fiber 2 Carbs 7
- Protein 7

KETOGENIC FISH AND

SEAFOOD RECIPES

22.   Incredible Salmon Rolls

This Asian dish is just delicious!

Preparation time: 10 minutes

Cooking time: 0 minutes

Servings: 12

Ingredients:

- 2 nori seeds

- 1 small avocado, pitted, peeled and finely
  chopped

- 6 ounces smoked salmon. Sliced

- 4 ounces cream cheese

- 1 cucumber, sliced

- 1 teaspoon wasabi paste

- Picked ginger for serving

Directions:

1. Place nori sheets on a sushi mat.

2. Divide salmon slices on them and also avocado and cucumber slices.

3. In a bowl, mix cream cheese with wasabi paste and stir well.

4. Spread this over cucumber slices, roll your nori sheets, press well, cut each in 6pieces and serve with pickled ginger.

Nutrition:

- Calories 80 Fat 6

- Fiber 1

- Carbs 2

- Protein 4

23.   Salmon Skewers

These are easy to make and they are very healthy!

Preparation time: 10 minutes

Cooking time: 8 minutes Servings: 4

Ingredients:

- 12 ounces salmon fillet, cubed
- 1 red onion, cut in chunks
- red bell pepper cut in chunks
- green bell pepper cut in chunks
- orange bell pepper cut in chunks
- Juice form 1 lemon
- Salt and black pepper to the taste
- A drizzle of olive oil

Directions:

1. Thread skewers with onion, red, green and

orange pepper and salmon cubes.

2. Season them with salt and pepper, drizzle oil and lemon juice and place them onpreheated grill over medium high heat.

3. Cook for 4 minutes on each side, divide on plates and serve.

Nutrition:

- Calories 150

- Fat 3

- Fiber 6

- Carbs 3

- Protein 8

24.   Grilled Shrimp

This is perfect! Just check it out!

Preparation time: 20 minutes

Cooking time: 10 minutes Servings: 4

Ingredients:

- 1 pound shrimp, peeled and deveined

- 1 tablespoon lemon juice

- 1 garlic clove, minced

-    cup basil leaves

- 1 tablespoon pine nuts, toasted

- 2 tablespoons parmesan, grated

- 2 tablespoons olive oil

- Salt and black pepper to the taste

Directions:

1. In your food processor, mix parmesan with basil,

garlic, pine nuts, oil, salt,pepper and lemon juice and blend well.

2. Transfer this to a bowl, add shrimp, toss to coat and leave aside for 20 minutes.

3. Thread skewers with marinated shrimp, place them on preheated grill overmedium high heat, cook for 3 minutes, flip and cook for 3 more minutes.

4. Arrange on plates and serve.

Nutrition:

- Calories 185
- Fat 11
- Fiber 0
- Carbs 2
- Protein 13

25.   **Calamari Salad**

It's an excellent choice for a summer day!

Preparation time: 30 minutes

Cooking time: 4 minutes

Servings: 4

Ingredients:

- 2 long red chilies, chopped

- 2 small red chilies, chopped

- 2 garlic cloves, minced

- 3 green onions, chopped

- 1 tablespoon balsamic vinegar

- Salt and black pepper to the taste

- Juice from 1 lemon

- 6 pounds calamari hoods, tentacles
  reserved o ounces olive oil

- 3 ounces rocket for serving

Directions:

1. In a bowl, mix long red chilies with small red chilies, green onions, vinegar, halfof the oil, garlic, salt, pepper and lemon juice and stir well.

2. Place calamari and tentacles in a bowl, season with salt and pepper, drizzle therest of the oil, toss to coat and place on preheated grill over medium high heat.

3. Cook for 2 minuets on each side and transfer to the chili marinade you've made.

4. Toss to coat and leave aside for 30 minutes.

5. Arrange rocket on plates, top with calamari and its marinade and serve.

Nutrition:

- Calories 200 Fat 4
- Fiber 2 Carbs 2
- Protein 7

26.   Cod Salad

It's always worth trying something new!

Preparation time: 2 hours and 10 minutes

Cooking time: 20 minutes

Servings: 8

Ingredients:

- 2 cups jarred pimiento peppers, chopped

- 2 pounds salt cod

- 1 cup parsley, chopped

- 1 cup kalamata olives, pitted and chopped

- 6 tablespoons capers

-     cup olive oil

- Salt and black pepper to the taste

- Juice from 2 lemons

- 4 garlic cloves, minced

- 2 celery ribs, chopped

- teaspoon red chili flakes

- 1 escarole head, leaves separated

Directions:

1. Put cod in a pot, add water to cover, bring to a boil over medium heat, boil for 20minutes, drain and cut into medium chunks.

2. Put cod in a salad bowl, add peppers, parsley, olives, capers, celery, garlic,lemon juice, salt, pepper, olive oil and chili flakes and toss to coat.

3. Arrange escarole leaves on a platter, add cod salad and serve.

Nutrition:

- Calories 240

- Fat 4 Fiber 2

- Carbs 6

- Protein 9

27.   Sardines Salad

It's a rich and nutritious winter salad you have to try soon!

Preparation time: 10 minutes

Cooking time: 0 minutes

Servings: 1

Ingredients:

- 5 ounces canned sardines in oil
- 1 tablespoons lemon juice
- 1 small cucumber, chopped
-   tablespoon mustard
- Salt and black pepper to the taste

Directions:

1. Drain sardines, put them in a bowl and mash using a fork.

2. Add salt, pepper, cucumber, lemon juice and mustard, stir well and serve cold.

Nutrition:

- Calories 200

- Fat 20

- Fiber 1

- Carbs 0

- Protein 20

KETOGENIC POULTRY RECIPES

28. So Delicious Chicken Wings

You will fall in love with this keto dish and you will make it over and over again!

Preparation time: 10 minutes Cooking time: 55 minutes Servings: 4

Ingredients:

- 3 pounds chicken wings
- Salt and black pepper to the taste
- 3 tablespoons coconut aminos
- 2 teaspoons white vinegar
- 3 tablespoons rice vinegar
- 3 tablespoons stevia

- cup scallions, chopped   teaspoon xantham gum 5 dried chilies, chopped

Directions:

1. Spread chicken wings on a lined baking sheet, season with salt and pepper,introduce in the oven at 375 degrees F and bake for 45 minutes.

2. Meanwhile, heat up a small pan over medium heat, add white vinegar, ricevinegar, coconut aminos, stevia, xantham gum, scallions and chilies, stir well,bring to a boil, cook for 2 minutes and take off heat.

3. Dip chicken wings into this sauce, arrange them all on the baking sheet againand bake for 10 minutes more.Serve them hot.

Nutrition:

calories 415 fat 23 fiber 3 carbs 2 protein 27

29.   Chicken In Creamy Sauce

Trust us! This keto recipe is here to impress you!

Preparation time: 10 minutes

Cooking time: 1 hour and 10 minutes

Servings: 4

Ingredients:

- 8 chicken thighs

- Salt and black pepper to the taste

- 1 yellow onion, chopped

- 1 tablespoon coconut oil

- 4 bacon strips, chopped

- 4 garlic cloves, minced

- 10 ounces cremimi mushrooms, halved

- 2 cups white chardonnay wine

- 1 cup whipping cream

- A handful parsley, chopped

Directions:

1. Heat up a pan with the oil over medium heat, add bacon, stir, cook until it'scrispy, take off heat and transfer to paper towels.

2. Heat up the pan with the bacon fat over medium heat, add chicken pieces, seasonthem with salt and pepper, cook until they brown and also transfer to papertowels.

3. Heat up the pan again over medium heat, add onions, stir and cook for 6minutes.

4. Add garlic, stir, cook for 1 minute and transfer next to bacon pieces.

5. Return pan to stove and heat up again over medium temperature.

6. Add mushrooms stir and cook them for 5 minutes.

7. Return chicken, bacon, garlic and onion to pan.

8. Add wine, stir, bring to a boil, reduce heat and simmer fro 40 minutes.

9. Add parsley and cream, stir and cook for 10 minutes more.

10. Divide on plates and serve.

Nutrition:

- Calories 340
- Fat 10
- Fiber 7
- Carbs 4
- Protein 24

30.   Delightful Chicken

It's a delicious and textured keto poultry dish!

Preparation time: 10 minutes

Cooking time: 1 hour

Servings: 4

Ingredients:

- 6 chicken breasts, skinless and boneless
- Salt and black pepper to the taste
- cup jalapenos, chopped
- 5 bacon slices, chopped
- 8 ounces cream cheese
- cup yellow onion, chopped
- cup mayonnaise
- cup parmesan, grated
- 1 cup cheddar cheese, grated
- For the topping:

- 2 ounces pork skins, crushed

- 4 tablespoons melted ghee

- cup parmesan

Directions:

1. Arrange chicken breasts in a baking dish, season with salt and pepper, introducein the oven at 425 degrees F and bake for 40 minutes.

2. Meanwhile, heat up a pan over medium heat, add bacon, stir, cook until it'scrispy and transfer to a plate.

3. Heat up the pan again over medium heat, add onions, stir and cook for 4minutes.

4. Take off heat, add bacon, jalapeno, cream cheese, mayo, cheddar cheese and cup parm and stir well..

5. Spread this over chicken.

6. In a bowl, mix pork skin with ghee and   cup parm and stir.

7. Spread this over chicken as well, introduce in the oven and bake for 15 minutesmore.

8. Serve hot.

Nutrition:

- Calories 340
- Fat 12
- Fiber 2
- Carbs 5
- Protein 20

31.   Tasty Chicken And Sour Cream Sauce

You've got to learn how to make this tasty keto dish! It's so tasty!

Preparation time: 10 minutes

Cooking time: 40 minutes Servings: 4

Ingredients:

- 4 chicken thighs
- Salt and black pepper to the taste
- 1 teaspoon onion powder
-    cup sour cream
- 2 tablespoons sweet paprika

Directions:

1. In a bowl, mix paprika with salt, pepper and onion powder and stir.

2. Season chicken pieces with this paprika mix, arrange them on a lined bakingsheet and bake in the oven at 400 degrees F for 40 minutes.

3. Divide chicken on plates and leave aside for now.

4. Pour juices from the pan into a bowl and add sour cream.

5. Stir this sauce very well and drizzle over chicken.

Nutrition:

- Calories 384
- Fat 31
- Fiber 2
- Carbs 1
- Protein 33

32.   Tasty Chicken Stroganoff

Have you heard about this keto recipe? It seems it's amazing!

Preparation time: 10 minutes

Cooking time: 4 hours and 10 minutes

Servings: 4

Ingredients:

- 2 garlic cloves, minced

- 8 ounces mushrooms, roughly chopped

-    teaspoon celery seeds, ground

- 1 cup chicken stock 1 cup coconut milk

- 1 yellow onion, chopped

- 1 pound chicken breasts, cut into medium pieces

- 1 and   teaspoons thyme, dried

- 2 tablespoons parsley, chopped

- Salt and black pepper to the tasted

- 4 zucchinis, cut with a spiralizer

Directions:

1. Put chicken in your slow cooker.

2. Add salt, pepper, onion, garlic, mushrooms, coconut milk, celery seeds, stock,half of the parsley and thyme.

3. Stir, cover and cook on High for 4 hours.

4. Uncover pot, add more salt and pepper if needed and the rest of the parsley andstir.

5. Heat up a pan with water over medium heat, add some salt, bring to a boil, addzucchini pasta, cook for 1 minute and drain.

6. Divide on plates, add chicken mix on top and serve.

Nutrition:

Calories 364 Fat 22 Fiber 2 Carbs 4 Protein 24

33.   Tasty Chicken Gumbo

Oh..you are going to love this!

Preparation time: 10 minutes

Cooking time: 7 hours

Servings: 5

Ingredients:

- 2 sausages, sliced

- 3 chicken breasts, cubed

- 2 tablespoons oregano, dried

- 2 bell peppers, chopped

- 1 small yellow onion, chopped

- 28 ounces canned tomatoes, chopped

- 3 tablespoons thyme, dried

- 2 tablespoons garlic powder

- 2 tablespoons mustard powder

- 1 teaspoon cayenne powder

- 1 tablespoons chili powder

- Salt and black pepper to the taste

- 6 tablespoons Creole seasoning

Directions:

1. In your slow cooker, mix sausages with chicken pieces, salt, pepper, bellpeppers, oregano, onion, thyme, garlic powder, mustard powder, tomatoes,cayenne, chili and Creole seasoning.

2. Cover and cook on Low for 7 hours.

3. Uncover pot again, stir gumbo and divide into bowls.

4. Serve hot.

Nutrition:

- Calories 360 Fat 23

- Fiber 2 Carbs 6

- Protein 23

KETOGENIC MEAT RECIPES

34.   Lavender Lamb Chops

It's amazing and very flavored! Try it as son as you can!

Preparation time: 10 minutes

Cooking time: 25 minutes

Servings: 4

Ingredients:

- 2 tablespoons rosemary, chopped

- 1 and   pounds lamb chops

- Salt and black pepper to the taste

- 1 tablespoon lavender, chopped

- 2 garlic cloves, minced

- 3 red oranges, cut in halves

- 2 small pieces of orange peel

- A drizzle of olive oil

- 1 teaspoon ghee

Directions:

1. In a bowl, mix lamb chops with salt, pepper, rosemary, lavender, garlic and orange peel, toss tocoat and leave aside for a couple of hours.

2. Grease your kitchen grill with ghee, heat up over medium high heat, place lamb chops on it, cookfor 3 minutes, flip, squeeze 1 orange half over them, cook for 3 minutes more, flip them again,cook them for 2 minutes and squeeze another orange half over them.

3. Place lamb chops on a plate and keep them warm for now..

4. Add remaining orange halves on preheated grill, cook them for 3 minutes, flip and cook them foranother 3 minutes.

5. Divide lamb chops on plates, add orange halves on the side, drizzle some olive oil over them andserve.

Nutrition:

- Calories 250
- Fat 5
- Fiber 1
- Carbs 5
- Protein 8

35. Crusted Lamb Chops

This is easy to make and it will taste very good!

Preparation time: 10 minutes

Cooking time: 15 minutes

Servings: 4

Ingredients:

- 2 lamb racks, cut into chops
- Salt and black pepper to the taste
- 3 tablespoons paprika
- cup cumin powder
- 1 teaspoon chili powder

Directions:

1. In a bowl, mix paprika with cumin, chili, salt and pepper and stir.
2. Add lamb chops and rub them well.

3. Heat up your grill over medium temperature, add lamb chops, cook for 5 minutes, flip and cookfor 5 minutes more.

4. Flip them again, cook for 2 minutes and then for 2 minutes more on the other side again.

Nutrition:

- Calories 200

- Fat 5

- Fiber 2

- Carbs 4

- Protein 8

36.   Lamb And Orange Dressing

You will love this dish!

Preparation time: 10 minutes

Cooking time: 4 hours Servings: 4

Ingredients:

- 2 lamb shanks

- Salt and black pepper to the taste

- 1 garlic head, peeled

- 4 tablespoons olive oil

- Juice from   lemon

- Zest from   lemon

-    teaspoon oregano, dried

Directions:

1. In your slow cooker, mix lamb with salt and
   pepper.

2. Add garlic, cover and cook on High for 4 hours.

3. Meanwhile, in a bowl, mix lemon juice with lemon zest, some salt and pepper, the olive oil andoregano and whisk very well.

4. Uncover your slow cooker, shred lamb meat and discard bone and divide on plates.

5. Drizzle the lemon dressing all over and serve.

Nutrition:

- Calories 160
- Fat 7
- Fiber 3
- Carbs 5
- Protein 12

37. Lamb Riblets And Tasty Mint Pesto

The pesto makes this keto dish really surprising and tasty!

Preparation time: 1 hour

Cooking time: 2 hours

Servings: 4

Ingredients:

- 1 cup parsley
- 1 cup mint
- 1 small yellow onion, roughly chopped
- 1/3 cup pistachios
- 1 teaspoon lemon zest
- 5 tablespoons avocado oil
- Salt to the taste
- 2 pounds lamb riblets

- onion, chopped

- 5 garlic cloves, minced

- Juice from 1 orange

Directions:

1. In your food processor, mix parsley with mint, 1 small onion, pistachios, lemon zest, salt andavocado oil and blend very well.

2. Rub lamb with this mix, place in a bowl, cover and leave in the fridge for 1 hour.

3. Transfer lamb to a baking dish, add garlic and onion to the dish as well, drizzle orange juiceand bake in the oven at 250 degrees F for 2 hours.

4. Divide on plates and serve.

Nutrition:

- Calories 200 Fat 4 Fiber 1 Carbs 5

- Protein 7

KETOGENIC VEGETABLE

RECIPES

38. Avocado And Cucumber Salad

You willask for more! It'ssuch a tastysummersalad!

Preparation time: 10 minutes

Cooking time: 0 minutes

Servings: 4

Ingredients:

- 1 smallredonion, sliced

- 1 cucumber, sliced

- 2 avocados, pitted, peeled and chopped

- 1 pound cherry tomatoes, halved

- 2 tablespoons olive oil

- cup cilantro, chopped

- 2 tablespoonslemonjuice

- Salt and black pepper to the taste

Directions:

1. In a large salad bowl, mix tomatoeswithcucumber, onion and avocado and stir.

2. Addoil, salt, pepper and lemonjuice and toss to coatwell.

3. Serve cold withcilantro on top.

Nutrition:

- Calories 140

- Fat 4

- Fiber 2

- Carbs 4

- Protein 5

39.   Delicious Avocado Soup

You will adore thisspecial and deliciousketosoup!

Preparation time: 10 minutes

Cooking time: 10 minutes

Servings: 4

Ingredients:

- 2 avocados, pitted, peeled and chopped

- 3 cups chicken stock

- 2 scallions, chopped

- Salt and black pepper to the taste

- 2 tablespoons ghee

- 2/3 cup heavycream

Directions:

1. Heat up a pot with the ghee over medium heat, addscallions, stir and cook for 2 minutes.

2. Add 2 and   cups stock, stir and simmer for 3 minutes.

3. In your blender, mix avocadoswith the rest of the stock, salt, pepper and heavycream and pulsewell.

4. Addthis to the pot, stirwell, cook for 2 minutes and seasonwith more salt and pepper.

5. Stirwell, ladleintosoup bowls and serve.

Nutrition:

- Calories 332
- Fat 23
- Fiber 4
- Carbs 6
- Protein 6

KETOGENIC DESSERT

RECIPES

40.   Chocolate Ganache

It willbedonein 5 minutes and it'scompletelyKetogenic!

Preparation time: 1 minute

Cooking time: 5 minutes Servings: 6

Ingredients:

- cup heavycream
- 4 ouncesdarkchocolate, unsweetened and chopped

Directions:

1. Put creaminto a pan and heat up over medium heat.

2. Take off heatwhenitbegins to simmer, addchocolatepieces and stiruntilitmelts.

3. Serve thisvery cold as a dessert or use it as a cream for a keto cake.

Nutrition:

- Calories 78
- Fat 1
- Fiber 1
- Carbs 2
- Protein 0